PIANO • VOCAL • GUITAR

THE BEST MOVIE SONGS EVER

D1243295

This publication is not for sale in
the E.C. and/or Australia
or New Zealand.

ISBN 0-7935-4765-2

7777 W. BLUEMOUND RD. P.O. BOX 13819 MILWAUKEE, WI 53213

CONTENTS
THE BEST MOVIE SONGS EVER

4. Alfie
ALFIE (1966)

8. Almost Paradise
FOOTLOOSE (1984)

12. Anniversary Song
THE JOLSON STORY (1946)

20. The Bare Necessities
THE JUNGLE BOOK (1965)

15. Beauty and the Beast
BEAUTY AND THE BEAST (1992)

24. Bless the Beasts and Children
BLESS THE BEASTS AND CHILDREN (1972)

28. Born Free
BORN FREE (1966)

30. Call Me Irresponsible
PAPA'S DELICATE CONDITION (1963)

34. Candle on the Water
PETE'S DRAGON (1977)

37. Chariots of Fire
CHARIOTS OF FIRE (1981)

40. Cheek to Cheek
TOP HAT (1935)

46. Chim Chim Cher-ee
MARY POPPINS (1964)

50. Circle of Life
THE LION KING (1994)

58. Come Saturday Morning
THE STERILE CUCKOO (1969)

61. The Continental
THE GAY DIVORCEE (1934)

68. A Dream Is a Wish Your Heart Makes
CINDERELLA (1950)

71. Endless Love
ENDLESS LOVE (1981)

76. Theme from E.T. (The Extra-Terrestrial)
E.T. (THE EXTRA-TERRESTRIAL) (1982)

81. Everybody's Talkin' (Echoes)
MIDNIGHT COWBOY (1969)

92. The Exodus Song
EXODUS (1960)

84. Flashdance...What a Feeling
FLASHDANCE (1983)

89. Funny Girl
FUNNY GIRL (1968)

97. Girl Talk
HARLOW (1965)

94. The Hands of Time
BRIAN'S SONG (1970)

100. I Will Wait for You
THE UMBRELLAS OF CHERBOURG (1964)

104. In the Still of the Night
ROSALIE (1937)

108. Isn't It Romantic?
LOVE ME TONIGHT (1932)

116. It Might As Well Be Spring
STATE FAIR (1945)

120. Theme from "Jaws"
JAWS (1975)

122. The John Dunbar Theme
DANCES WITH WOLVES (1990)

124. Theme from "Jurassic Park"
JURASSIC PARK (1994)

113. Theme from "Lawrence of Arabia"
LAWRENCE OF ARABIA (1962)

128. Let's Face the Music and Dance
FOLLOW THE FLEET (1936)

132. Long Ago (And Far Away)
COVER GIRL (1944)

135. The Look of Love
CASINO ROYALE (1967)

138. Love Letters
LOVE LETTERS (1983)

142. Love Theme
CINEMA PARADISO (1989)

145. A Man and a Woman
A MAN AND A WOMAN (1966)

148. The Man That Got Away
A STAR IS BORN (1954)

154. Maybe This Time
CABARET (1972)

151. Moon River
BREAKFAST AT TIFFANY'S (1961)

158. Moonlight Becomes You
ROAD TO MOROCCO (1942)

162. The Music of Goodbye
OUT OF AFRICA (1985)

166. My Foolish Heart
MY FOOLISH HEART (1949)

168. Pennies from Heaven
PENNIES FROM HEAVEN (1936)
PENNIES FROM HEAVEN (1981)

176. Picnic
PICNIC (1956)

178. Puttin' on the Ritz
PUTTIN' ON THE RITZ (1930)

182. Que Sera, Sera (Whatever Will Be, Will Be)
THE MAN WHO KNEW TOO MUCH (1955)

186. Raiders March
RAIDERS OF THE LOST ARK (1981)

190. Raindrops Keep Fallin' on My Head
**BUTCH CASSIDY AND THE SUNDANCE KID
(1969)**

173. River
THE MISSION (1986)

194. Theme from "Schindler's List"
SCHINDLER'S LIST (1994)

196. Separate Lives
WHITE NIGHTS (1985)

204. Somewhere Out There
AN AMERICAN TAIL (1986)

212. Sooner or Later (I Always Get My Man)
DICK TRACY (1990)

218. Speak Softly, Love (Love Theme)
THE GODFATHER (1972)

209. Star Trek® - The Motion Picture
STAR TREK (1979)

220. Steppin' Out With My Baby
EASTER PARADE (1948)

224. Summertime in Venice
SUMMERTIME (1955)

227. Take My Breath Away (Love Theme)
TOP GUN (1986)

232. Tears in Heaven
RUSH (1991)

240. Theme from "Terms of Endearment"
TERMS OF ENDEARMENT (1983)

246. Thanks for the Memory
BIG BROADCAST OF 1938

250. That's Entertainment
THE BAND WAGON (1953)

237. A Time for Us (Love Theme)
ROMEO AND JULIET (1968)

254. True Love
HIGH SOCIETY (1956)

256. Unchained Melody
UNCHAINED (1955)
GHOST (1990)

260. Up Where We Belong
AN OFFICER AND A GENTLEMAN (1982)

264. The Way We Were
THE WAY WE WERE (1973)

267. The Way You Look Tonight
SWING TIME (1936)

270. Where Do I Begin (Love Theme)
LOVE STORY (1970)

274. Where the Boys Are
WHERE THE BOYS ARE (1961)

277. A Whole New World (Aladdin's Theme)
ALADDIN (1993)

284. Zip-A-Dee-Doo-Dah
SONG OF THE SOUTH (1946)

ALFIE
Theme from the Paramount Picture ALFIE

Words by HAL DAVID
Music by BURT BACHARACH

Very Slowly, Rubato

Lyrics: What's it all a-bout, Al - fie?___ Is it just for the mo - ment we live? What's it all a-bout___ when you sort it out,___ Al - fie?___

ALMOST PARADISE
Love Theme from the Paramount Motion Picture FOOTLOOSE

Words by DEAN PITCHFORD
Music by ERIC CARMEN

ANNIVERSARY SONG
from THE JOLSON STORY

By AL JOLSON and SAUL CHAPLIN

BEAUTY AND THE BEAST
from Walt Disney's BEAUTY AND THE BEAST

Lyrics by HOWARD ASHMAN
Music by ALAN MENKEN

THE BARE NECESSITIES
from Walt Disney's THE JUNGLE BOOK

Words and Music by
TERRY GILKYSON

Look for the bare ne - ces - si - ties, the

sim - ple bare ne - ces - si - ties; ___ for - get a - bout your

wor - ries and your strife.

I mean the
I mean the
I mean the

bare ne - ces - si - ties, ___ or Moth - er Na - ture's
bare ne - ces - si - ties, ___ that's why a bear can
bare ne - ces - si - ties, ___ or Moth - er Na - ture's

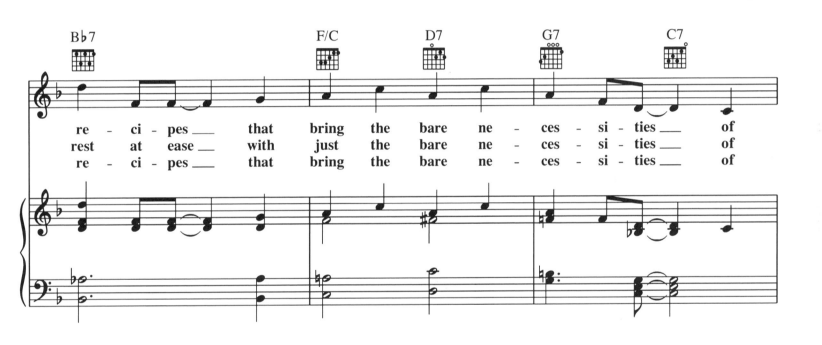

re - ci - pes ___ that bring the bare ne - ces - si - ties ___ of
rest at ease ___ with just the bare ne - ces - si - ties ___ of
re - ci - pes ___ that just bring the bare ne - ces - si - ties ___ of

life. ___ Wher - ev - er I wan - der, ___
life. ___ When you ___ pick a paw - paw
life. ___ So just try to re - lax *(Oh Yeah!)*

F   C7

___ wher - ev - er I roam.   I could - n't be fond - er ___
___ or pric-kl - y pear.   And you_ prick a raw paw, ___
___ in my back yard.   If you act like that bee acts ___

F   F7   Bb

___ of my big home.   The bees are buzz - in' in the
___ next time be - ware.   Don't pick the prick - ly pear by
___ you're work-in' too hard.   Don't spend your time just look-in' a -

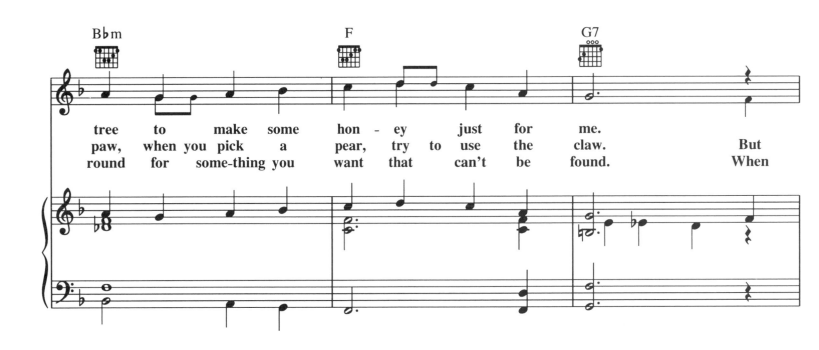

Bbm   F   G7

tree to make some hon - ey just for me.   But
paw, when you pick a pear, try to use the claw.   When
round for some-thing you want that can't be found.   When

BLESS THE BEASTS AND CHILDREN
from BLESS THE BEASTS AND CHILDREN

Words and Music by BARRY DeVORZON
and PERRY BOTKIN, JR.

BORN FREE

from the Columbia Pictures' Release BORN FREE

Words by DON BLACK
Music by JOHN BARRY

CALL ME IRRESPONSIBLE
from the Paramount Picture PAPA'S DELICATE CONDITION

Words by SAMMY CAHN
Music by JAMES VAN HEUSEN

CANDLE ON THE WATER
from Walt Disney's PETE'S DRAGON

Words and Music by AL KASHA
and JOEL HIRSCHHORN

Lyrics:

I'll be your can-dle on the wa-ter,
My love for you will al-ways burn.
I know you're lost and drift-ing,
But the clouds are lift-ing,
don't give up you have some-where to turn.

I'll be your can-dle on the wa-ter,
'Til ev-'ry wave is warm and bright,
My soul is there be-side you,
Let this can-dle guide you,
soon you'll see a gold-en stream of light.

CHARIOTS OF FIRE
from CHARIOTS OF FIRE

Music by VANGELIS

CHEEK TO CHEEK
from the RKO Radio Motion Picture TOP HAT

Words and Music by
IRVING BERLIN

CHIM CHIM CHER-EE
from Walt Disney's MARY POPPINS

Words and Music by RICHARD M. SHERMAN
and ROBERT B. SHERMAN

CIRCLE OF LIFE
from Walt Disney Pictures' THE LION KING

Music by ELTON JOHN
Lyrics by TIM RICE

Moderately, with an African beat

Same tempo, gently rhythmic

(*African chant continues*)

COME SATURDAY MORNING

(a/k/a SATURDAY MORNING)
from the Paramount Picture THE STERILE CUCKOO

Words by DORY PREVIN
Music by FRED KARLIN

THE CONTINENTAL

from THE GAY DIVORCEE

Words by CON CONRAD
Music by HERBERT MAGIDSON

A DREAM IS A WISH YOUR HEART MAKES

from Walt Disney's CINDERELLA

Words and Music by MACK DAVID,
AL HOFFMAN and JERRY LIVINGSTON

Moderately

When I was a lit-tle {girl, boy,} my fa-ther used to say, if trou-ble ev-er trou-bles you, just dream your cares a-way. A dream is a wish your heart makes ___

ENDLESS LOVE

from ENDLESS LOVE

Words and Music by
LIONEL RICHIE

Moderately Slow

My love, there's on-ly you in my life, the on-ly thing that's right.
Two hearts, two hearts that beat as one; our lives have just be-gun.

My first love, you're ev-'ry breath that I take, you're ev-'ry
For-ev-er, I'll hold you close in my arms, I can't re-

74

THEME FROM E.T.
(THE EXTRA-TERRESTRIAL)
from the Universal Picture E.T. (THE EXTRA-TERRESTRIAL)

Music by JOHN WILLIAMS

Piano Solo

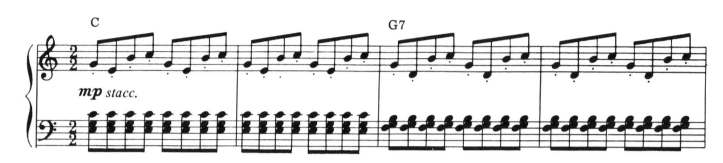

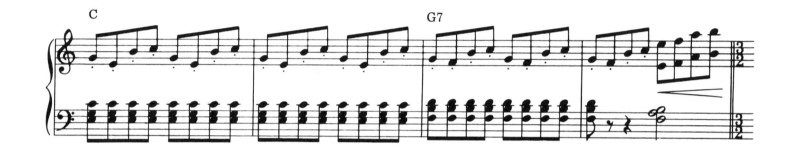

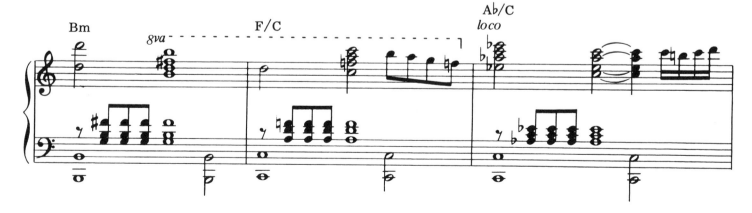

EVERYBODY'S TALKIN'
(ECHOES)
from MIDNIGHT COWBOY

Words and Music by
FRED NEIL

skip-pin' o - ver the o - cean like a stone.____

D.S. al Coda

CODA

And

I won't let you leave my love ___ be - hind.__

Repeat and Fade

And

FLASHDANCE...WHAT A FEELING

from the Paramount Picture FLASHDANCE

Lyrics by KEITH FORSEY and IRENE CARA
Music by GIORGIO MORODER

FUNNY GIRL
from FUNNY GIRL

Words by BOB MERRILL
Music by JULE STYNE

THE EXODUS SONG
from EXODUS

Words by PAT BOONE
Music by ERNEST GOLD

THE HANDS OF TIME
Theme from the Screen Gems Television Production BRIAN'S SONG

Words by ALAN and MARILYN BERGMAN
Music by MICHEL LEGRAND

GIRL TALK
from the Paramount Picture HARLOW

Words by BOBBY TROUP
Music by NEAL HEFTI

I WILL WAIT FOR YOU
from THE UMBRELLAS OF CHERBOURG

Music by MICHEL LEGRAND
Original French Text by JACQUES DEMY
English Lyrics by NORMAN GIMBEL

IN THE STILL OF THE NIGHT

from ROSALIE

Words and Music by
COLE PORTER

Moderate Beguine Tempo

Mysteriously

In The Still Of The Night,_____

As I gaze from my win - dow,

At the moon in its flight, My thoughts all

ISN'T IT ROMANTIC?
from the Paramount Picture LOVE ME TONIGHT

Words by LORENZ HART
Music by RICHARD RODGERS

I've nev-er met you, yet nev-er
My face is glow-ing, I'm en-er-

doubt, dear, I can't for-get you, I've thought you
get-ic, the art of sew-ing, I found po-

out, dear. I know your pro-file and I know the way you
et-ic. My nee-dle punc-tu-ates the rhy-thm of ro-

THEME FROM
"LAWRENCE OF ARABIA"

from LAWRENCE OF ARABIA

By MAURICE JARRE

IT MIGHT AS WELL BE SPRING

from STATE FAIR

Lyrics by OSCAR HAMMERSTEIN II
Music by RICHARD RODGERS

THEME FROM "JAWS"
from the Universal Picture JAWS

By JOHN WILLIAMS

THE JOHN DUNBAR THEME
from DANCES WITH WOLVES

By JOHN BARRY

Very slowly

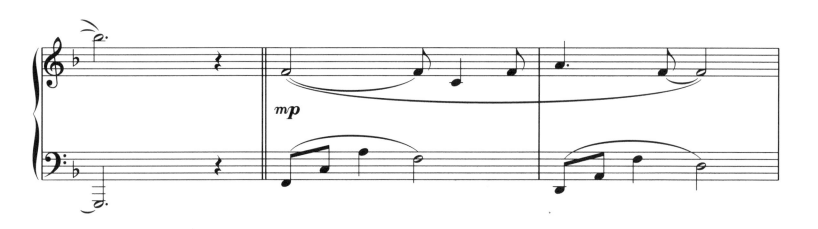

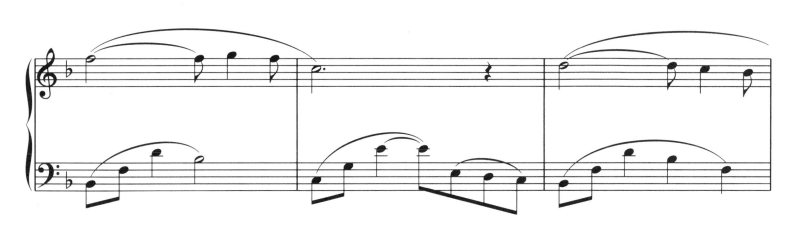

THEME FROM "JURASSIC PARK"

from the Universal Motion Picture JURASSIC PARK

Composed by JOHN WILLIAMS

LET'S FACE THE MUSIC AND DANCE

from the Motion Picture FOLLOW THE FLEET

Words and Music by
IRVING BERLIN

LONG AGO
(AND FAR AWAY)
from COVER GIRL

Words by IRA GERSHWIN
Music by JEROME KERN

Moderately slow

Long a - go and far a - way, I
dreamed a dream one day and now that
dream is here be - side me. Long the

THE LOOK OF LOVE

from CASINO ROYALE

Words by HAL DAVID
Music by BURT BACHARACH

LOVE LETTERS
Theme from the Paramount Picture LOVE LETTERS

Words by EDWARD HEYMAN
Music by VICTOR YOUNG

Moderately slow, with expression

The sky may be star - less, the night may be moon - less, but deep in my heart there's a glow, _____ for

LOVE THEME
from CINEMA PARADISO

Music by
ANDREA MORRICONE

A MAN AND A WOMAN
(UN HOMME ET UNE FEMME)
from A MAN AND A WOMAN

Original Words by PIERRE BAROUH
English Words by JERRY KELLER
Music by FRANCIS LAI

THE MAN THAT GOT AWAY

from the Motion Picture A STAR IS BORN

Lyric by IRA GERSHWIN
Music by HAROLD ARLEN

Slowly, but insistently

MOON RIVER
from the Paramount Picture BREAKFAST AT TIFFANY'S

Words by JOHNNY MERCER
Music by HENRY MANCINI

MAYBE THIS TIME
from CABARET

Lyric by FRED EBB
Music by JOHN KANDER

Maybe this time — I'll be luck-y. — Maybe this time he'll stay.

Maybe this time, — For the first time, — love won't hur-ry a-way.

He will hold me fast.

MOONLIGHT BECOMES YOU

from the Paramount Picture ROAD TO MOROCCO

Words by JOHNNY BURKE
Music by JAMES VAN HEUSEN

THE MUSIC OF GOODBYE
Love Theme from OUT OF AFRICA

Music by JOHN BARRY
Words by ALAN and MARILYN BERGMAN

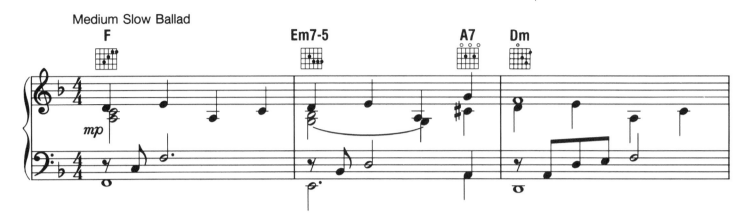

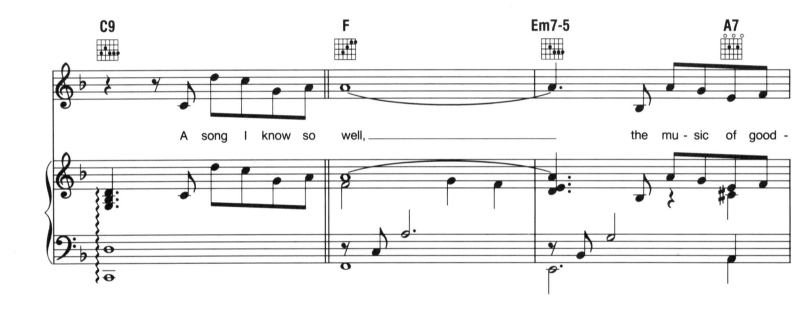

A song I know so well, _____ the mu-sic of good-

bye a - gain. _____ It's there each time we say "hel - lo." _____

MY FOOLISH HEART
from MY FOOLISH HEART

Words by NED WASHINGTON
Music by VICTOR YOUNG

Slowly and expressively

PENNIES FROM HEAVEN

from PENNIES FROM HEAVEN

Words by JOHN BURKE
Music by ARTHUR JOHNSTON

RIVER
from the Motion Picture THE MISSION

Music by ENNIO MORRICONE

Moderately

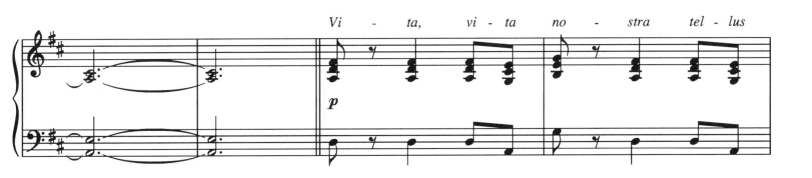

Vi - ta, vi - ta no - stra tel - lus

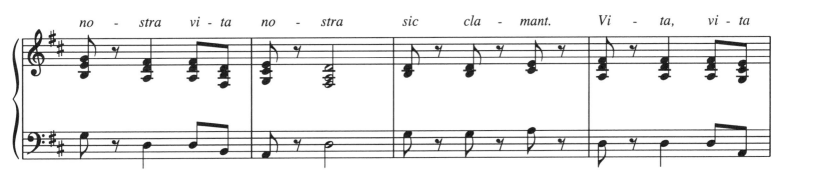

no - stra vi - ta no - stra sic cla - mant. Vi - ta, vi - ta

no - stra tel - lus no - stra vi - ta no - stra sic cla - mant.

174

PICNIC
from the Columbia Technicolor Picture PICNIC

Words by STEVE ALLEN
Music by GEORGE W. DUNING

PUTTIN' ON THE RITZ
from the Motion Picture PUTTIN' ON THE RITZ

Words and Music by
IRVING BERLIN

Lyrics:
Have you seen the well-to-do __ up and down Park Av-e-nue, __ on that fam-ous thor-ough-fare __ with their nos-es in the air. __ High hats and

QUE SERA, SERA
(WHATEVER WILL BE, WILL BE)
from THE MAN WHO KNEW TOO MUCH

Words and Music by
JAY LIVINGSTON
and RAY EVANS

RAIDERS MARCH
from the Paramount Motion Picture RAIDERS OF THE LOST ARK

By JOHN WILLIAMS

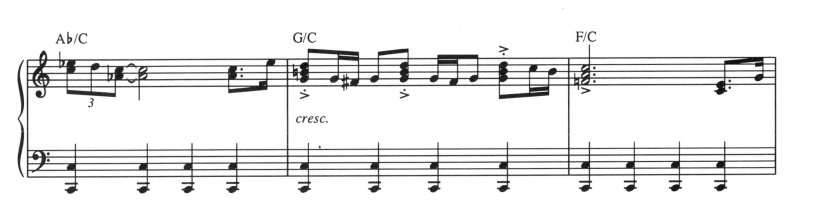

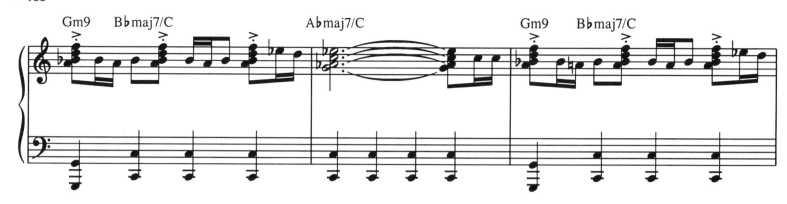

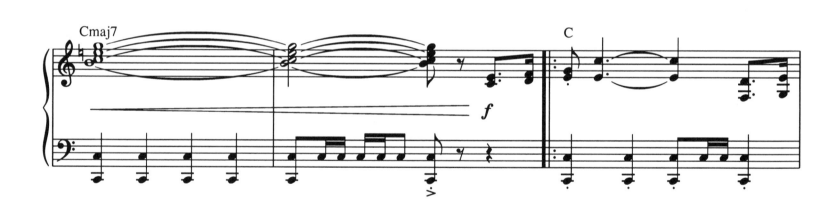

RAINDROPS KEEP FALLIN' ON MY HEAD

from BUTCH CASSIDY AND THE SUNDANCE KID

Lyric by HAL DAVID
Music by BURT BACHARACH

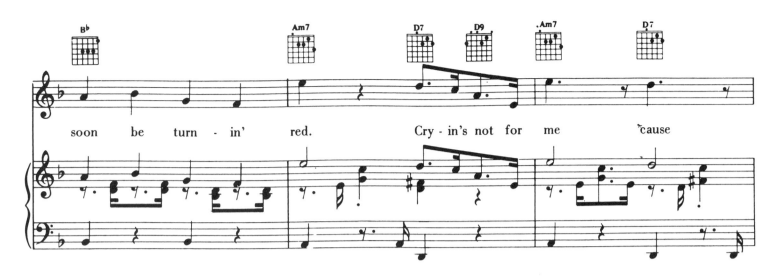

soon be turn - in' red.   Cry - in's not for me   'cause

I'm   nev - er gon - na stop the rain   by com-plain-in'.   Be - cause I'm

free   noth - in's wor - ry - in'   me._____

THEME FROM "SCHINDLER'S LIST"

from the Universal Motion Picture SCHINDLER'S LIST

Composed by JOHN WILLIAMS

MCA music publishing

SEPARATE LIVES
Love Theme from WHITE NIGHTS

Words and Music by
STEPHEN BISHOP

SOMEWHERE OUT THERE

from AN AMERICAN TAIL

Words and Music by JAMES HORNER,
BARRY MANN and CYNTHIA WEIL

Moderately, with expression

STAR TREK® - THE MOTION PICTURE

Theme from the Paramount Picture STAR TREK

Music by JERRY GOLDSMITH

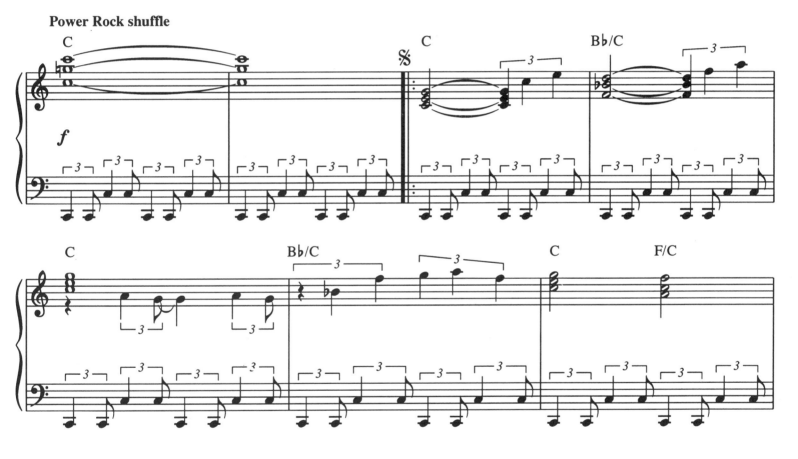

SOONER OR LATER
(I ALWAYS GET MY MAN)
from the Film DICK TRACY

Words and Music by
STEPHEN SONDHEIM

Slow Swing, with a steady beat

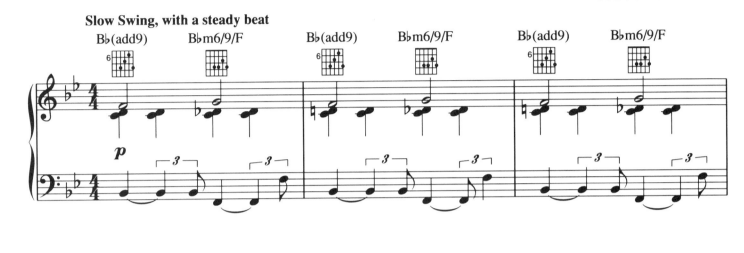

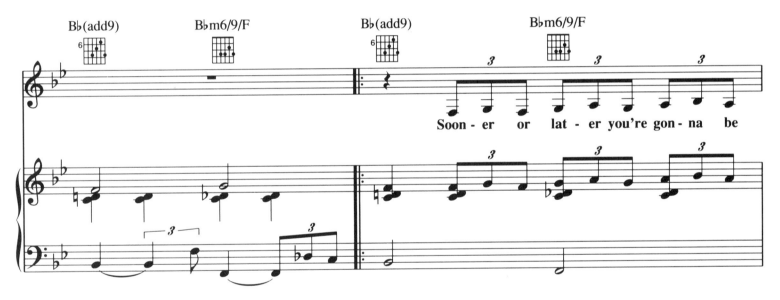

Soon - er or lat - er you're gon - na be

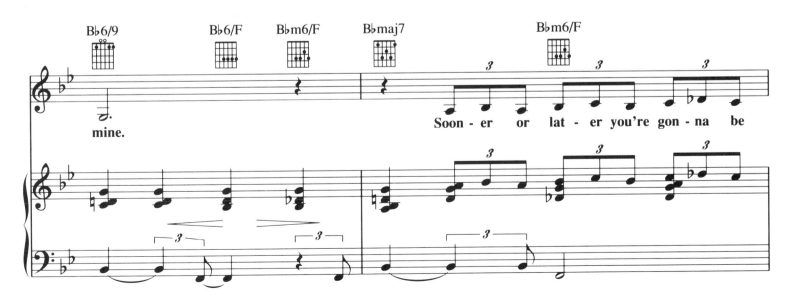

mine.

Soon - er or lat - er you're gon - na be

SPEAK SOFTLY, LOVE
(LOVE THEME)
from the Paramount Picture THE GODFATHER

Words by LARRY KUSIK
Music by NINO ROTA

Speak soft-ly, love, and hold me warm a-gainst your heart. I feel your words, the ten-der, trem-bling mo-ments start. We're in a world our ver-y own, shar-ing a love that on-ly few have ev-er known. Wine col-ored

STEPPIN' OUT WITH MY BABY

from the Motion Picture Irving Berlin's EASTER PARADE

Words and Music by
IRVING BERLIN

SUMMERTIME IN VENICE
from the Motion Picture SUMMERTIME

English Words by CARL SIGMAN
Music by ICINI

TAKE MY BREATH AWAY
(LOVE THEME)
from the Paramount Picture TOP GUN

Words and Music by GIORGIO MORODER
and TOM WHITLOCK

TEARS IN HEAVEN
Featured in the Motion Picture RUSH

Words and Music by ERIC CLAPTON
and WILL JENNINGS

A TIME FOR US
(LOVE THEME)
from the Paramount Picture ROMEO AND JULIET

Words by LARRY KUSIK and EDDIE SNYDER
Music by NINO ROTA

THEME FROM "TERMS OF ENDEARMENT"

from the Paramount Picture TERMS OF ENDEARMENT

By MICHAEL GORE

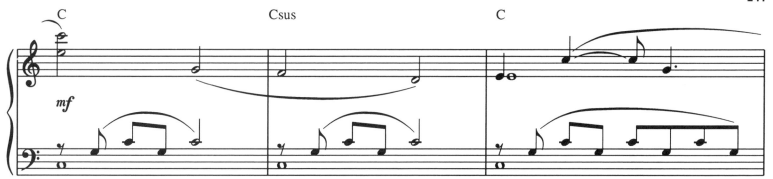

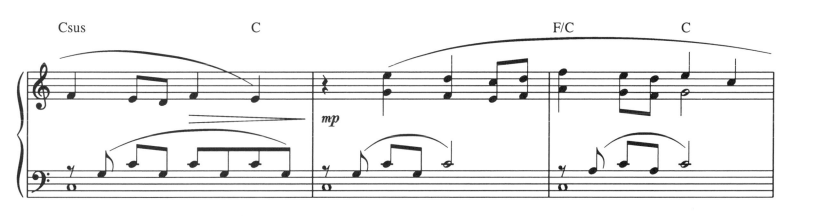

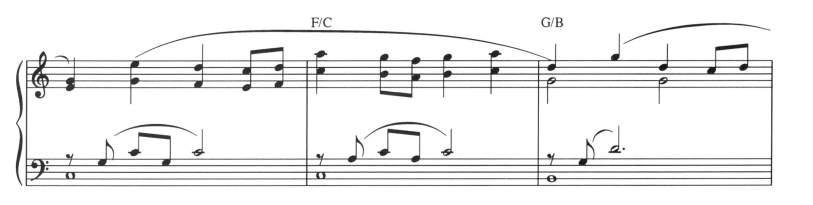

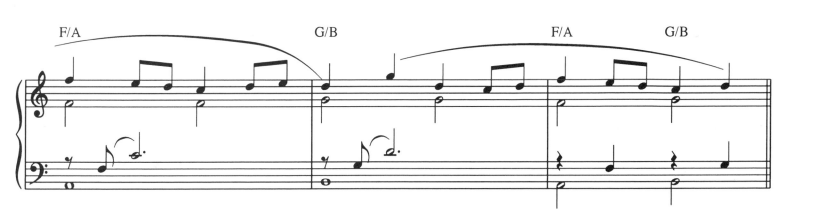

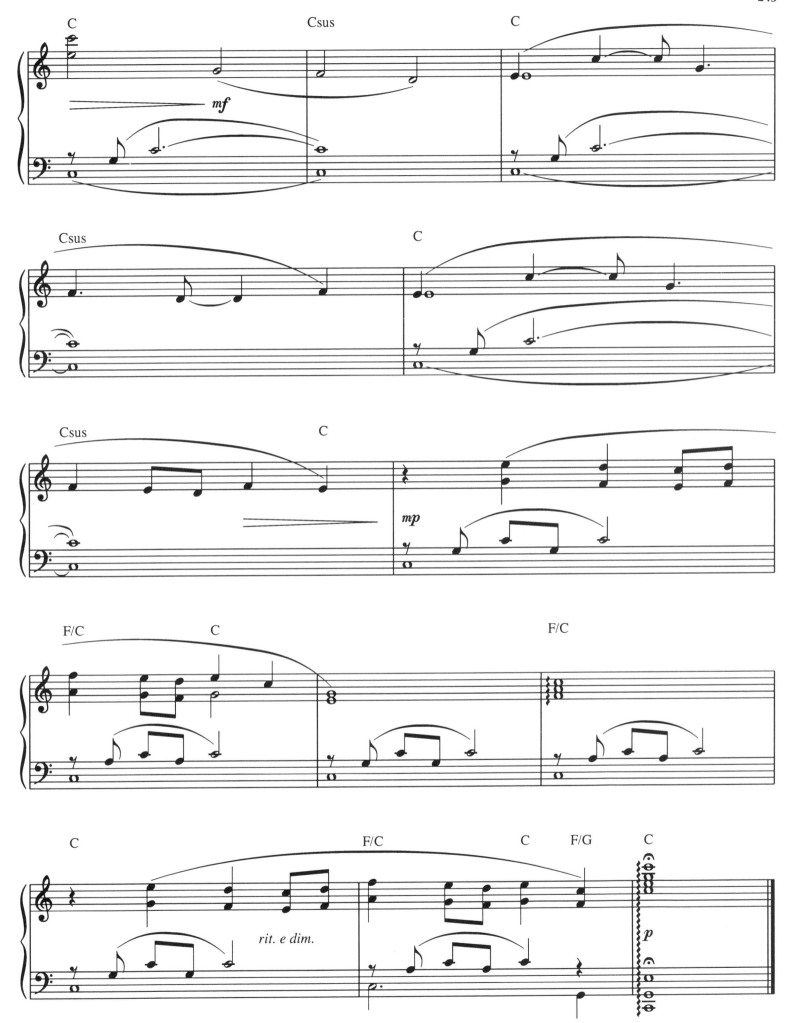

THANKS FOR THE MEMORY

from the Paramount Picture BIG BROADCAST OF 1938

Words and Music by LEO ROBIN
and RALPH RAINGER

THAT'S ENTERTAINMENT
from THE BAND WAGON

Words by HOWARD DIETZ
Music by ARTHUR SCHWARTZ

TRUE LOVE
from HIGH SOCIETY

Words and Music by
COLE PORTER

Moderately Slow

UNCHAINED MELODY

from the Motion Picture UNCHAINED
Featured in the Motion Picture GHOST

Lyric by HY ZARET
Music by ALEX NORTH

UP WHERE WE BELONG

from the Paramount Picture AN OFFICER AND A GENTLEMAN

Words by WILL JENNINGS
Music by BUFFY SAINTE-MARIE and JACK NITZSCHE

THE WAY WE WERE

from the Motion Picture THE WAY WE WERE

Words by ALAN and MARILYN BERGMAN
Music by MARVIN HAMLISCH

THE WAY YOU LOOK TONIGHT
from SWING TIME

Words by DOROTHY FIELDS
Music by JEROME KERN

Andantino

Some — day ___ when I'm aw - f'ly low, When the world is
love - ly, With your smile so warm, And your cheek so

cold, I will feel a glow just think - ing of you
soft, There is noth - ing for me but to love you,

And the way you look to - night. _____
Just the way you look to - night. _____

Oh, but you're

WHERE DO I BEGIN

(LOVE THEME)

from the Paramount Picture LOVE STORY

Words by CARL SIGMAN
Music by FRANCIS LAI

Where do I be-gin _____ to tell the sto-ry of how
With her first hel-lo _____ she gave a mean-ing to this

great a love can be, _____ the sweet love sto-ry that is
emp-ty world of mine. _____ There'd nev-er be an-oth-er

old-er than the sea, the sim-ple truth a-bout the
love, an-oth-er time; she came in-to my life and

WHERE THE BOYS ARE

Featured in the Motion Picture WHERE THE BOYS ARE

Words and Music by HOWARD GREENFIELD
and NEIL SEDAKA

A WHOLE NEW WORLD
(ALADDIN'S THEME)
from Walt Disney's ALADDIN

Music by ALAN MENKEN
Lyrics by TIM RICE

ZIP-A-DEE-DOO-DAH
from Walt Disney's SONG OF THE SOUTH

Words by RAY GILBERT
Music by ALLIE WRUBEL

Additional Lyrics

2. Zip-a-dee-doo-dah, Zip-a-dee-ay,
   My, oh my, what a wonderful day.
   Plenty of sunshine headin' our way.
   We never doubted he'd get away.
   Movin' on taught him a lesson,
   You learned it well Brer Rabbit,
   Getting caught's a nasty habit.
   Zip-a-dee-doo-dah, zip-a-dee-ay
     wonderful feeling, feeling this way.
   (To Bridge)

3. Zip-a-dee-doo-dah, Zip-a-dee-ay,
   Brer Fox and Brer Bear gonna get it today.
   Zip-a-dee-doo-dah, Zip-a-dee-ay,
   That hungry gator's getting his way,
   Mister Bluebird on my shoulder
   It's the truth it's actual
   Everything is satisfactual.
   Zip-a-dee-doo-dah, Zip-a-dee-ay,
   Wonderful feeling, wonderful day.

The Greatest Songs Ever Written

The Best Ever Collection

Arranged for Piano, Voice & Guitar

150 Of The Most Beautiful Songs Ever

Over 400 pages of slow and sentimental ballads, including: Come In From The Rain • Edelweiss • The First Time Ever I Saw Your Face • For All We Know • How Deep Is Your Love • I Have Dreamed • I'll Be Seeing You • If We Only Have Love • Love Is Blue • Red Roses For A Blue Lady • Songbird • Summertime • Unchained Melody • Yesterday, When I Was Young • Young At Heart • many more.
00360735 ....$19.95

The Best Big Band Songs Ever

69 of the greatest big band songs ever, including: Ballin' The Jack • Basin Street Blues • Boogie Woogie Bugle Boy • The Continental • Don't Get Around Much Anymore • In The Mood • Let A Smile Be Your Umbrella • Marie • Moonglow • Opus One • Satin Doll • Sentimental Journey • String Of Pearls • Who's Sorry Now.
00359129 ....$15.95

The Best Broadway Songs Ever

Over 65 songs in all! Highlights include: All I Ask Of You • As Long As He Needs Me • Bess, You Is My Woman • Bewitched • Camelot • Climb Ev'ry Mountain • Comedy Tonight • Don't Cry For Me Argentina • Everything's Coming Up Roses • Getting To Know You • I Could Have Danced All Night • I Dreamed A Dream • If I Were A Rich Man • The Last Night Of The World • Love Changes Everything • Oklahoma! • Ol' Man River • People • Try To Remember • and many more!
00309155 ……................................$17.95

The Best Christmas Songs Ever

A collection of 72 of the most-loved songs of the season, including: Blue Christmas • The Chipmunk Song • Frosty The Snow Man • A Holly Jolly Christmas • Home For The Holidays • I'll Be Home For Christmas • Jingle-Bell Rock • Let It Snow ! Let It Snow ! Let It Snow! • Parade Of The Wooden Soldiers • Rudolph, The Red-Nosed Reindeer • Santa, Bring Back My Baby (To Me) • Silver Bells • Suzy Snowflake • Toyland.
00359130 ...…...............................$17.95

The Best Country Songs Ever

Over 65 songs, featuring: Always On My Mind • Behind Closed Doors • Could I Have This Dance • Crazy • Daddy Sang Bass • D-I-V-O-R-C-E • Forever And Ever, Amen • God Bless The U.S.A. • Grandpa (Tell Me 'Bout The Good Old Days) • Help Me Make It Through The Night • I Fall To Pieces • Mammas Don't Let Your Babies Grow Up To Be Cowboys • Stand By Your Man • Through The Years • and more.
00359135 ....$16.95

The Best Easy Listening Songs Ever

A collection of 75 mellow favorites, featuring: All Out Of Love • Can't Smile Without You • (They Long To Be) Close To You • Every Breath You Take • Eye In The Sky • How Am I Supposed To Live Without You • I Dreamed A Dream • Imagine • Love Takes Time • Piano Man • The Rainbow Connection • Sing • Vision Of Love • Your Song.
00359193 ....$15.95

The Best Jazz Standards Ever

77 of the greatest jazz hits of all time, including: April In Paris • Body And Soul • Don't Get Around Much Anymore • I Got It Bad And That Ain't Good • I've Got You Under My Skin • It Don't Mean A Thing (If It Ain't Got That Swing) • Love Is Here To Stay • Misty • Out Of Nowhere • Satin Doll • Unforgettable • When I Fall In Love • and many more.
00311641 ....$17.95

The Best Love Songs Ever

A collection of 66 favorite love songs, including: The Anniversary Song • (They Long To Be) Close To You • Endless Love • Here And Now • Just The Way You Are • Longer • Love Takes Time • Misty • My Funny Valentine • So In Love • You Needed Me • Your Song.
00359198 ....$17.95

The Best Movie Songs Ever

Over 70 songs, including: Alfie • Beauty And The Beast • Born Free • Endless Love • Theme From "Jurassic Park" • Moon River • Somewhere Out There • Tears In Heaven • A Whole New World • and more.
00310063 ....$19.95

The Best Rock Songs Ever

70 songs, including: All Day And All Of The Night • All Shook Up • Ballroom Blitz • Bennie And The Jets • Blue Suede Shoes • Born To Be Wild • Boys Are Back In Town • Every Breath You Take • Faith • Free Bird • Hey Jude • Lola • Louie, Louie • Maggie May • Money • We Got The Beat • Wild Thing • more!
00490424 ....$16.95

The Best Songs Ever – Revised

Over 70 must-own classics, including: All I Ask Of You • Body And Soul • Crazy • Endless Love • In The Mood • Love Me Tender • Memory • Moonlight In Vermont • My Funny Valentine • People • Satin Doll • Save The Best For Last • Somewhere Out There • Strangers In The Night • Tears In Heaven • A Time For Us • The Way We Were • When I Fall In Love • You Needed Me • and more.
00359224 ....$19.95

The Best Standards Ever

Volume 1 (A-L)

72 beautiful ballads, including: All The Things You Are • Bewitched • Don't Get Around Much Anymore • Getting To Know You • God Bless' The Child • Hello, Young Lovers • It's Only A Paper Moon • I've Got You Under My Skin • The Lady Is A Tramp • Little White Lies.
00359231 ....$15.95

Volume 2 (M-Z)

72 songs, including: Makin' Whoopee • Misty • Moonlight In Vermont • My Funny Valentine • Old Devil Moon • The Party's Over • People Will Say We're In Love • Smoke Gets In Your Eyes • Strangers In The Night • Tuxedo Junction • Yesterday.
00359232 ....$15.95

FOR MORE INFORMATION, SEE YOUR LOCAL MUSIC DEALER,
OR WRITE TO:

HAL•LEONARD™
CORPORATION
7777 W. BLUEMOUND RD. P.O. BOX 13819 MILWAUKEE, WI 53213

Prices, contents and availability subject to change without notice. Not all products available outside the U.S.A.

0995

Classic Collections Of Your Favorite Songs

arranged for piano, voice, and guitar.

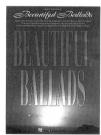

Beautiful Ballads

A massive collection of 87 songs, including: April In Paris • Autumn In New York • Call Me Irresponsible • Cry Me A River • I Wish You Love • I'll Be Seeing You • If • Imagine • Isn't It Romantic? • It's Impossible (Somos Novios) • Mona Lisa • Moon River • People • The Way We Were • A Whole New World (Aladdin's Theme) • and more.

00311679 ....$17.95

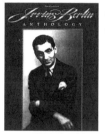

Irving Berlin Anthology

A comprehensive collection of 61 timeless songs with a bio, song background notes, and photos. Songs include: Always • Blue Skies • Cheek To Cheek • God Bless America • Marie • Puttin' On The Ritz • Steppin' Out With My Baby • There's No Business Like Show Business • White Christmas • (I Wonder Why?) You're Just In Love • and more.

00312493 ....$19.95

The Best Standards Ever Volume 1 (A-L)

72 beautiful ballads, including: All The Things You Are • Bewitched • Can't Help Lovin' Dat Man • Don't Get Around Much Anymore • Getting To Know You • God Bless' The Child • Hello, Young Lovers • I Got It Bad And That Ain't Good • It's Only A Paper Moon • I've Got You Under My Skin • The Lady Is A Tramp • Little White Lies.

00359231 ....$15.95

The Best Standards Ever Volume 2 (M-Z)

72 songs, including: Makin' Whoopee • Misty • Moonlight In Vermont • My Funny Valentine • Old Devil Moon • The Party's Over • People Will Say We're In Love • Smoke Gets In Your Eyes • Strangers In The Night • Tuxedo Junction • Yesterday.

00359232 ....$15.95

The Big Book Of Standards

86 classics essential to any music library, including: April In Paris • Autumn In New York • Blue Skies • Cheek To Cheek • Heart And Soul • I Left My Heart In San Francisco • In The Mood • Isn't It Romantic? • Mona Lisa • Moon River • The Nearness Of You • Out Of Nowhere • Spanish Eyes • Star Dust • Stella By Starlight • That Old Black Magic • They Say It's Wonderful • What Now My Love • and more.

00311667 ....$19.95

The Hal Leonard Family Song Album

Over 100 songs arranged for piano, organ, guitar and all "C" instruments. Only the best-remembered and most-requested songs since the turn of the century are featured – from "Sidewalks Of New York" to "You Needed Me." Major song eras represented are: Broadway; big band; hits of the '20s; '30s; '40s; '50s; country; inspirational. Two handy song indexes provided – alphabetical by song title and by song category. A special narrative on each song is also featured, providing insight into the circumstances surrounding its creation.

00240334 ....$17.95

I'll Be Seeing You: 50 Songs Of World War II

A salute to the music and memories of WWII, including a year-by-year chronology of events on the homefront, dozens of photos, and 50 radio favorites of the GIs and their families back home, including: Boogie Woogie Bugle Boy • Don't Sit Under The Apple Tree (With Anyone Else But Me) • I Don't Want To Walk Without You • I'll Be Seeing You • Moonlight In Vermont • There's A Star-Spangled Banner Waving Somewhere • You'd Be So Nice To Come Home To • and more.

00311698 ....$19.95

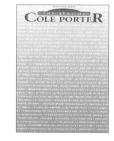

Best Of Cole Porter

38 of his classics, including: All Of You • Anything Goes • Be A Clown • Don't Fence Me In • I Get A Kick Out Of You • In The Still Of The Night • Let's Do It (Let's Fall In Love) • Night And Day • You Do Something To Me • and many more.

00311577 ....$14.95

Remember This One?

43 classics, including: Ac-cent-tchu-ate The Positive • Ain't She Sweet • Autumn Leaves • (The Original) Boogie Woogie • A Good Man Is Hard To Find • I Wanna Be Loved By You • Mister Sandman • Sentimental Journey • Sioux City Sue • Unchained Melody • and more.

00384600 ....$12.95

The Best Of Rodgers & Hammerstein

A capsule of 26 classics from this legendary duo. Songs include: Climb Ev'ry Mountain • Edelweiss • Getting To Know You • I'm Gonna Wash That Man Right Outa My Hair • My Favorite Things • Oklahoma • The Surrey With The Fringe On Top • You'll Never Walk Alone • and more.

00308210 ....$12.95

The Best Songs Ever – Revised

80 must-own classics, including: All I Ask Of You • Body And Soul • Crazy • Endless Love • Fly Me To The Moon • Here's That Rainy Day • In The Mood • Love Me Tender • Memory • Moonlight In Vermont • My Funny Valentine • People • Satin Doll • Save The Best For Last • Somewhere Out There • Strangers In The Night • Tears In Heaven • A Time For Us • The Way We Were • When I Fall In Love • You Needed Me • and more.

00359224 .... $19.95

Torch Songs

Sing your heart out with this collection of 59 sultry jazz and big band melancholy masterpieces, including: Angel Eyes • Cry Me A River • I Can't Get Started • I Got It Bad And That Ain't Good • I'm Glad There Is You • Lover Man (Oh, Where Can You Be?) • Misty • My Funny Valentine • Stormy Weather • and many more! 224 pages.

00490446 ....$14.95

Prices, contents, and availability subject to change without notice.
Some products may be unavailable outside the U.S.A.

FOR MORE INFORMATION, SEE YOUR LOCAL MUSIC DEALER,
OR WRITE TO:

HAL•LEONARD CORPORATION

7777 W. BLUEMOUND RD. P.O. BOX 13819 MILWAUKEE, WI 53213